Paris
Notebook

Images/drawings © Fabrice Moireau
Text © Roger Williams

© Editions Didier Millet
121 Telok Ayer Street #03-01
Singapore 068590

Designed by Annie Teo

Printed in Singapore by Tien Wah Press

ISBN: 978-981-4385-82-4

www.edmbooks.com
www.leseditionsdupacifique.com

Paris
Notebook

Paintings Fabrice Moireau

EDITIONS
DIDIER
MILLET

Personal data

Name :
Address :

Telephone :
Fax :
Mobile :
E-mail :

Work address :

Telephone :
Fax :
E-mail :

Paris

Paris has a reputation as a city of romance, culture, cuisine and style. And visitors arriving with such expectations are rarely disappointed. It has long held its place as one of Europe's most engaging capitals, helped by the harmony of its architecture which changed little in a century. Unchanged, too, are the distinctive districts that have their own shops, styles and flavours.

The site on the River Seine, 120 km (75 miles) from the sea, has been inhabited since the Stone Age, and it was the Celtic tribe of the Parisii, settling on the Île de la Cité, who gave the city its name. This island is where the massive Gothic cathedral of Nôtre Dame now stands. The Romans later occupied the island and they built a temple

to Mercury on Montmartre – the hill on which martyr St Denis, first bishop of Paris, was decapitated. The hill is now better known for its nightspots such as Moulin Rouge and Lapin Agile, which attracted Toulous-Lautrec, Picasso and the fashionable of the Belle Époque.

The city grew up in two parts. The intellectual Left Bank, on the southern side of the Seine, was where the Sorbonne university and the École des Beaux Arts were established, and where the 20th-century's left-wing thinkers and writers met in cafés such as Les Deux Magots and Café de Flore, and in the jazz clubs of Montparnasse, while Ernest Hemingway and just about every romantic lost soul of the time headed for Shakespeare and Company, a celebrated bookstore. It was on the Left Bank that Marie de Médicis, Queen of France and second wife of Henri IV, rebuilt the Palace of Luxembourg in 1625 to remind her of her Florentine home. Clovis, first king of the Franks and founder of the city, was buried nearby, beneath the Abbey of St Genevieve, now the Panthéon.

The Right Bank, on the north side of the river, is for royalty, government, high-end shopping, opera houses and *grands boulevards*, laid out during Baron Haussmann's reform of the city in the mid-19th century. Originally a fortress, the Louvre was a palace from the 1360s until the French Revolution, after which it became a museum. It started as a

depository for national art treasures, and expanded to collections acquired by Napoleon during his military campaigns. Opposite is the Palais-Royale, built for Louis XIII's chief minister, Cardinal Richelieu, and now a quiet corner of the city, while the Élysée Palace, once home of Napoleon, is where the French President lives.

Napoleon is remembered in the Arc de Triomphe on the Champs Elysées, scene of celebrations at the end of World War II after the occupying German army retreated, its commanding officer bravely defying orders from Berlin to raze the city to the ground. One of the biggest annual celebrations in Paris is Bastille Day, 14 July, commemorating the storming of the Bastille, a prison, at the start of the French Revolution in 1789. The Bastille district is on the eastern side of the city, near the Marais, the old Jewish quarter and a place of delightful cafés and bars. Narrow cobbled lanes lead to *hôtels* – enormous mansions which the nobles built in the 17th century, that today provide space for the Picasso Museum, Paris Historical Museum, etc.

South of the Marais is Île de St Louis, one of two natural islands in the River Seine, smaller than the neighbouring Île de la Cité. Although it's sitting in the heart of the city, the island has a quiet, village air, confirming Paris as a chic city with a soft heart.

View from the Centre Georges-Pompidou

Statue of Danton,
Latin Quarter,
Historic Centre

Place de la Madeleine,
8th arrondissement,
Western Paris

Alexander-III bridge,
Western Paris

Rue Manin,
19th arrondissement,
Northern Paris

Belleville, Eastern Paris

Paris' main Chinatown,
13th arrondissement,
Southern Paris

View from
Rue Berthe,
Montmartre,
Northern Paris

Rue Norvins, Montmartre, Northern Paris

2015

January

Mon	Tue	Wed	Thu	Fri	Sat	Sun
			1	2	3	4
5	6	7	8	9	10	11
12	13	14	15	16	17	18
19	20	21	22	23	24	25
26	27	28	29	30	31	

February

Mon	Tue	Wed	Thu	Fri	Sat	Sun
						1
2	3	4	5	6	7	8
9	10	11	12	13	14	15
16	17	18	19	20	21	22
23	24	25	26	27	28	

March

Mon	Tue	Wed	Thu	Fri	Sat	Sun
30	31					1
2	3	4	5	6	7	8
9	10	11	12	13	14	15
16	17	18	19	20	21	22
23	24	25	26	27	28	29

April

Mon	Tue	Wed	Thu	Fri	Sat	Sun
		1	2	3	4	5
6	7	8	9	10	11	12
13	14	15	16	17	18	19
20	21	22	23	24	25	26
27	28	29	30			

May

Mon	Tue	Wed	Thu	Fri	Sat	Sun
				1	2	3
4	5	6	7	8	9	10
11	12	13	14	15	16	17
18	19	20	21	22	23	24
25	26	27	28	29	30	31

June

Mon	Tue	Wed	Thu	Fri	Sat	Sun
1	2	3	4	5	6	7
8	9	10	11	12	13	14
15	16	17	18	19	20	21
22	23	24	25	26	27	28
29	30					

July

Mon	Tue	Wed	Thu	Fri	Sat	Sun
		1	2	3	4	5
6	7	8	9	10	11	12
13	14	15	16	17	18	19
20	21	22	23	24	25	26
27	28	29	30	31		

August

Mon	Tue	Wed	Thu	Fri	Sat	Sun
31					1	2
3	4	5	6	7	8	9
10	11	12	13	14	15	16
17	18	19	20	21	22	23
24	25	26	27	28	29	30

September

Mon	Tue	Wed	Thu	Fri	Sat	Sun
	1	2	3	4	5	6
7	8	9	10	11	12	13
14	15	16	17	18	19	20
21	22	23	24	25	26	27
28	29	30				

October

Mon	Tue	Wed	Thu	Fri	Sat	Sun
			1	2	3	4
5	6	7	8	9	10	11
12	13	14	15	16	17	18
19	20	21	22	23	24	25
26	27	28	29	30	31	

November

Mon	Tue	Wed	Thu	Fri	Sat	Sun
30						1
2	3	4	5	6	7	8
9	10	11	12	13	14	15
16	17	18	19	20	21	22
23	24	25	26	27	28	29

December

Mon	Tue	Wed	Thu	Fri	Sat	Sun
	1	2	3	4	5	6
7	8	9	10	11	12	13
14	15	16	17	18	19	20
21	22	23	24	25	26	27
28	29	30	31			

2016

January

Mon	Tue	Wed	Thu	Fri	Sat	Sun
				1	2	3
4	5	6	7	8	9	10
11	12	13	14	15	16	17
18	19	20	21	22	23	24
25	26	27	28	29	30	31

February

Mon	Tue	Wed	Thu	Fri	Sat	Sun
1	2	3	4	5	6	7
8	9	10	11	12	13	14
15	16	17	18	19	20	21
22	23	24	25	26	27	28
29						

March

Mon	Tue	Wed	Thu	Fri	Sat	Sun
	1	2	3	4	5	6
7	8	9	10	11	12	13
14	15	16	17	18	19	20
21	22	23	24	25	26	27
28	29	30	31			

April

Mon	Tue	Wed	Thu	Fri	Sat	Sun
				1	2	3
4	5	6	7	8	9	10
11	12	13	14	15	16	17
18	19	20	21	22	23	24
25	26	27	28	29	30	

May

Mon	Tue	Wed	Thu	Fri	Sat	Sun
30	31					1
2	3	4	5	6	7	8
9	10	11	12	13	14	15
16	17	18	19	20	21	22
23	24	25	26	27	28	29

June

Mon	Tue	Wed	Thu	Fri	Sat	Sun
		1	2	3	4	5
6	7	8	9	10	11	12
13	14	15	16	17	18	19
20	21	22	23	24	25	26
27	28	29	30			

July

Mon	Tue	Wed	Thu	Fri	Sat	Sun
				1	2	3
4	5	6	7	8	9	10
11	12	13	14	15	16	17
18	19	20	21	22	23	24
25	26	27	28	29	30	31

August

Mon	Tue	Wed	Thu	Fri	Sat	Sun
1	2	3	4	5	6	7
8	9	10	11	12	13	14
15	16	17	18	19	20	21
22	23	24	25	26	27	28
29	30	31				

September

Mon	Tue	Wed	Thu	Fri	Sat	Sun
			1	2	3	4
5	6	7	8	9	10	11
12	13	14	15	16	17	18
19	20	21	22	23	24	25
26	27	28	29	30		

October

Mon	Tue	Wed	Thu	Fri	Sat	Sun
31					1	2
3	4	5	6	7	8	9
10	11	12	13	14	15	16
17	18	19	20	21	22	23
24	25	26	27	28	29	30

November

Mon	Tue	Wed	Thu	Fri	Sat	Sun
	1	2	3	4	5	6
7	8	9	10	11	12	13
14	15	16	17	18	19	20
21	22	23	24	25	26	27
28	29	30				

December

Mon	Tue	Wed	Thu	Fri	Sat	Sun
			1	2	3	4
5	6	7	8	9	10	11
12	13	14	15	16	17	18
19	20	21	22	23	24	25
26	27	28	29	30	31	

2017

January

Mon	Tue	Wed	Thu	Fri	Sat	Sun
30	31					1
2	3	4	5	6	7	8
9	10	11	12	13	14	15
16	17	18	19	20	21	22
23	24	25	26	27	28	29

February

Mon	Tue	Wed	Thu	Fri	Sat	Sun
		1	2	3	4	5
6	7	8	9	10	11	12
13	14	15	16	17	18	19
20	21	22	23	24	25	26
27	28					

March

Mon	Tue	Wed	Thu	Fri	Sat	Sun
		1	2	3	4	5
6	7	8	9	10	11	12
13	14	15	16	17	18	19
20	21	22	23	24	25	26
27	28	29	30	31		

April

Mon	Tue	Wed	Thu	Fri	Sat	Sun
					1	2
3	4	5	6	7	8	9
10	11	12	13	14	15	16
17	18	19	20	21	22	23
24	25	26	27	28	29	30

May

Mon	Tue	Wed	Thu	Fri	Sat	Sun
1	2	3	4	5	6	7
8	9	10	11	12	13	14
15	16	17	18	19	20	21
22	23	24	25	26	27	28
29	30	31				

June

Mon	Tue	Wed	Thu	Fri	Sat	Sun
			1	2	3	4
5	6	7	8	9	10	11
12	13	14	15	16	17	18
19	20	21	22	23	24	25
26	27	28	29	30		

July

Mon	Tue	Wed	Thu	Fri	Sat	Sun
31					1	2
3	4	5	6	7	8	9
10	11	12	13	14	15	16
17	18	19	20	21	22	23
24	25	26	27	28	29	30

August

Mon	Tue	Wed	Thu	Fri	Sat	Sun
	1	2	3	4	5	6
7	8	9	10	11	12	13
14	15	16	17	18	19	20
21	22	23	24	25	26	27
28	29	30	31			

September

Mon	Tue	Wed	Thu	Fri	Sat	Sun
				1	2	3
4	5	6	7	8	9	10
11	12	13	14	15	16	17
18	19	20	21	22	23	24
25	26	27	28	29	30	

October

Mon	Tue	Wed	Thu	Fri	Sat	Sun
30	31					1
2	3	4	5	6	7	8
9	10	11	12	13	14	15
16	17	18	19	20	21	22
23	24	25	26	27	28	29

November

Mon	Tue	Wed	Thu	Fri	Sat	Sun
		1	2	3	4	5
6	7	8	9	10	11	12
13	14	15	16	17	18	19
20	21	22	23	24	25	26
27	28	29	30			

December

Mon	Tue	Wed	Thu	Fri	Sat	Sun
				1	2	3
4	5	6	7	8	9	10
11	12	13	14	15	16	17
18	19	20	21	22	23	24
25	26	27	28	29	30	31

Rue du Calvaire, 18th arrondissement, Montmartre, Northern Paris

Paris at a glance

Official name: Paris

Country: France

Also known as: City of Light (a name the city earned during the Age of Enlightenment)

Location: Situated on the River Seine, at the heart of the Île-de-France region, Northern France

Coordinates: 48°51'24"N 2°21'03"E

Land area: 105.4 sq km (41 sq miles)

Population: Approx 2.25 million in the city, 12 million in the metropolitan city

Main religion: Roman Catholicism

Language spoken: French

Currency: Euro

Time zone: CET (UTC +1)

International dialing code: +33-1

Main airport: Paris-Charles de Gaulle Airport (one of the busiest in the world)

UNESCO World Heritage Sites: Banks of the Seine, Palace and Park of Versailles, Fontainebleau

Most well-known landmarks: the Eiffel Tower, the Louvre, Arc de Triomphe, Nôtre-Dame de Paris, Basilique du Sacré-Cœur, Musée d'Orsay, Musée Rodin, Musée Picasso

Fun things to do: Honeymoon, visit museums, watch operas, stroll along the River Seine and enjoy a cup of coffee with a *pain au chocolat* in a terrace café, attend a French dessert cookery class, find and taste the best wines in the city, take a day trip to Chartres, the medieval city one hour from Paris by car or by train

Best known literature: *The Hunchback of Notre Dame*, *Les Misérables* (both by Victor Hugo)

Useful phrases: *Salut/Bonjour* (Hello), *Ça va?/Comment ça va?* (How are you?), *Merci/Merci beaucoup* (thank you), *Bon appétit!* (Enjoy your meal!), *Au revoir/À bientôt* (Goodbye)

Website: www.paris.fr

The watercolours of Fabrice Moireau, which illustrate this notebook, have been published by Editions Didier Millet in *Paris Sketchbook*, *Gardens of Paris Sketchbook* and *Rooftops of Paris*.

Other titles in this series:

ARTIST **Fabrice Moireau**
Loire Valley Sketchbook
New York Sketchbook
Provence Sketchbook
Rome Sketchbook
Venice Sketchbook

ARTIST **A. Kasim Abas**
Sarawak Sketchbook

ARTIST **Graham Byfield**
Amsterdam Sketchbook
Bahamas Sketchbook
Bali Sketchbook
London Sketchbook
Oxford Sketchbook
Singapore Sketchbook

ARTIST **Chin Kon Yit**
Kuala Lumpur: A Sketchbook
Landmarks of Malaysia
Landmarks of Perak (with
A. Kasim Abas and Huai-yan Chang)
Landmarks of Selangor
Malacca Sketchbook
Penang Sketchbook

ARTIST **Sophie Ladame**
Mauritius Sketchbook

ARTIST **Taveepong Limapornvanich**
Thailand Sketchbook

For more information please log on
to: www.edmbooks.com